I0459155

The Skilled Sower

EMMANUEL ADEWUSI

CCCG Publishing House

Author: Emmanuel Adewusi

ISBN: 978-1-989099-44-5 (hardcover)

ISBN: 978-1-989099-45-2 (ebook)

First Printing 2025

Contents

Dedication

This book is dedicated to those who have lost their lives while taking the gospel of Jesus Christ to dangerous locations.

It is dedicated to those who are busy on the harvest field, doing all it takes, to bring in the harvest of souls into the kingdom of God.

It is dedicated to God, the most skilled sower, from whom we are all learning how to sow effectively.

Preface

If there is something that every born-again Christian knows they **ought to do**, but struggle with doing is telling others about Jesus Christ and why they need him.

Evangelism is a misunderstood subject in the body of Christ. When I make this statement, I am not referring to the mechanics of evangelism, I am referring to the effectiveness of evangelism. I often find believers celebrating the fact that someone boldly preached salvation in a public place, more than when a lost soul comes to Christ. Many believers are stuck wishing they were bold enough to preach salvation in a public place, rather than paying attention to the effectiveness of the method of evangelism.

Do we measure the success of evangelism by the boldness of the evangelist, its perceived effectiveness, or whether it made an impact at all? Ultimately, success isn't about audacity alone but about whether the message was delivered with the power of the Holy Spirit. These questions and much more will be answered in this book.

I have read many great books on evangelism and I believe God will use this book to perfect the body of Christ in this sacrosanct act of evangelism.

Introduction

Knowing where to go, but not knowing how to effectively get there, can be frustrating. This is because, *"the labor of fools wearies them, for they do not even know how to go to the city!"* (Ecclesiastes 10:15)

Preaching the gospel to unbelievers is only a means to an end. The end goal is what Jesus Christ told us in Matthew 28:18, *"Go therefore and make disciples of all the nations, baptizing them in the name of the Father and of the Son and of the Holy Spirit."* The moment we place excessive emphasis on preaching the gospel without giving thought to its effectiveness, we are setting ourselves up for frustration. Making disciples is the end goal, and we must keep that as our focus.

An experienced farmer knows that a good seed that has been sown will faced all sorts of oppositions to its ability to become fruitful. The opposition will come from both flora and fauna, as well as environmental and human factors. However, a skilled farmer anticipates these obstacles and is well equipped to overcome them successfully.

The parable in Mark 4 shows us different results from evangelistic efforts. From this parable, we can see what negatively affects the soul winning efforts. If we can understand those factors and learn how to scripturally mitigate them, we will be more effective in soul winning. Contrary to common interpretations, this parable does not suggest the inevitability of lost souls; rather, it reveals why souls are lost, enabling us to develop godly strategies to minimize those losses.

Join me as we draw principles from the scriptures that will make our evangelistic efforts to be fruitful.

1

Evangelism is for All Believers

WHAT IS EVANGELISM?

Evangelism refers to the act of sharing the gospel with those who does not believe. Any activity aimed solely at communicating the gospel to non-believers is considered evangelistic. If an activity does not ultimately result in the gospel being shared with unbelievers, it cannot be classified as evangelism.

WHY SHOULD YOU EVANGELIZE?

God is not a taskmaster. He does not ask us to do things that are burdensome or impossible. He always accompanies His instructions with promises and blessings. For example, Deuteronomy 28 starts with a clear instruction followed by a promise: *"Now it shall come to pass, if you diligently obey the voice of the Lord your God and carefully observe all His commandments which I command you today, that the Lord your God will set you high above all nations of the earth."* The Bible continues to outline the blessings that come from obedience.

Here are three reasons why we should share the good news of the gospel with others:

It is a Demonstration of Your Love for Jesus

Jesus Christ has instructed every child of God to share the good news of the Kingdom of God with others. If we truly love Jesus, we will share the gospel with others. Love is not just a tingling feeling we have towards someone; it is an active choice. Jesus said, *"If you love me, obey my commandments."* (John 14:15, NLT) This means that if we do not obey His instructions, we do not truly love Him.

We often refer to God's instruction to tell others about the good news of the kingdom of God as **the Great Commission**.

- And He said to them, *"Go into all the world and preach the gospel to every creature."* (Mark 16:15)

- *And Jesus came and spoke to them, saying, "All authority has been given to Me in heaven and on earth. Go therefore and make disciples of all the nations, baptizing them in the name of the Father and of the Son and of the Holy Spirit, teaching them to observe all things that I have commanded you; and lo, I am with you always, even to the end of the age." Amen* (Matthew 28:18-20)

- *"You did not choose Me, but I chose you, and appointed you that you should go and bear fruit, and that your fruit should remain."* (John 15:16)

Every believer must share the good news of the Kingdom of God out of obedience as a demonstration of their love for Jesus Christ.

In return for genuinely displaying our love for God, He promises to shower us with unimaginable blessings. The Bible tells us in 1 Corinthians 2:9, *"But as it is written: 'Eye has not seen, nor ear heard, nor have entered into the heart of man the things which God has prepared for those who love Him."* Imagine God pouring His blessings on you in this profound way! As you display your love for Jesus Christ by obeying His instruction to share the gospel with others, expect blessings that exceed anything you can imagine.

Giving to God is good; praise and worship are valuable, but sharing the good news of Jesus Christ with others is even better. God first demonstrated His love for humanity by giving His only begotten Son, Jesus Christ, to die on the cross for our sins. The question is, how are you demonstrating your love for God? As David stated in 1 Chronicles 21:24, *"No, but I will surely buy it for the full price; for I will not take what is yours for the Lord, nor offer burnt offerings with that which costs me nothing."*

Sharing your faith may lead to the loss of certain relationships and can sometimes bring pain, persecution, rejection, and hurt. However, remember that in all things, we are more than conquerors (Romans 8:37). Like David, you should boldly declare that you will not serve God at no cost to yourself.

We live in a time when it is unlikely we will experience the severe physical pain that early Christians faced while sharing their faith. Many of us will never be fed to lions, thrown into a blazing furnace, burned alive, or crucified for our beliefs. However, there is always a price to pay to demonstrate our love for Jesus Christ. This is why Jesus said in Matthew 10:38, *"And he who does not take his cross and follow after Me is not worthy of Me."*

The "cross" Jesus referred to symbolizes the personal sacrifices we must make to follow Him.

Receive Answers to Prayers

Do you want your prayers to be answered? Would you like a direct line to heaven? If your answer is yes, the key lies in committing yourself to share the gospel with others and ensuring that those who accept the gospel are properly discipled. Jesus Christ has promised us direct access to God for answered prayers when we share the good news of the kingdom and disciple those who embrace the message of salvation.

"You did not choose Me, but I chose you and appointed you that you should go and bear fruit, and that your fruit should remain, that whatever you ask the Father in My name He may give you." (John 15:16)

We are also instructed in Matthew 6:33, *"But seek first the kingdom of God and His righteousness, and all these things shall be added to you."* You can pray for your needs and desires, but when you prioritize the welfare and expansion of God's kingdom, God Himself will bless your life with both your needs and wants.

When you are seeking after God, you won't crave material possessions. He has promised that when you seek His kingdom, He will provide not just for your basic needs but also for your desires. As expressed in Psalm 23:1, *"The Lord is my Shepherd; I shall not want,"* which can also be interpreted as *"The Lord is my Shepherd; I shall not be in want."*

Assurance of Signs and Wonders

This refers to God's visible and tangible presence in a person's life. You can pray for signs and wonders to be evident in your life and ministry, but you must actively partner with God in sharing the gospel in order to experience these signs and wonders.

"So then, after the Lord had spoken to them, He was received up into heaven and sat down at the right hand of God. And they went out and preached everywhere, the Lord working with them and confirming the word through the accompanying signs. Amen." (Mark 16:19-20)

In this passage, we see that signs and wonders accompanied the Apostles as they preached the gospel of Jesus Christ. It is important to note that the Lord Jesus Christ was working alongside them to bring about these signs and wonders. This demonstrates how simple it can be to witness signs and wonders when actively involved in spreading the gospel.

2

Types of Evangelism

According to Jeremiah 16:16, there are primarily two types of evangelism. **You are either evangelizing as a hunter or a fisherman**. To be effective, every skilled sower should function in these two capacities.

"Behold, I will send for many fishermen," says the Lord, "and they shall fish them; and afterward I will send for many hunters, and they shall hunt them from every mountain and every hill, and out of the holes of the rocks." (Jeremiah 16:16)

HUNTING

Hunting is when you are sowing the seeds of the gospel alone, i.e. not in partnership with other believers. A skilled sower must be able to pursue unbelievers one-on-one. Like a hunter who operates independently to pursue prey, an evangelist in this role must be versatile and adaptable in their approach.

Jesus Christ operated as a hunter during His earthly ministry. We see Him target the Samaritan woman in John 4 where He single-handedly preached the gospel to her. We also see in that same passage that the Samaritan woman went into the city as a hunter to win souls to Jesus Christ.

Many believers are more comfortable when evangelizing as part of a group. While this is an acceptable way to evangelize, we must make sure that we are also able to preach to unbelievers individually.

A hunter must possess certain key characteristics to be successful.

Characteristics of an Effective Hunter

Patience

It is not unusual to see a hunter crouch quietly in an inconspicuous place, waiting for the perfect opportunity to strike. The same goes for the skilled sower that is utilizing the hunting technique while sowing.

You have to be willing to wait for as long as it would take to present the gospel to the unbeliever. If the hunter hastily delivers the gospel message to the unbeliever, it can hamper, or potentially ruin the possibility of the unbeliever ever responding to the gospel.

Knowledge of the Terrain and Prey

A good hunter must have a deep understanding of both their prey and the environment it operates. In choosing who will be sent to certain individuals, God usually chooses those that are well aware of the terrain that the unbeliever operates. God demonstrated the importance of this in sending Apostle Paul to the Gentiles, while He sent Apostle Peter to the Jews.

God may send a person to their own tribe, an academic to fellow scholars, a mathematician to other mathematicians, or a medical practitioner to colleagues in the field.

Endurance

A good hunter must have endurance. Unlike large-scale fishing, where multiple fish can be caught at once, hunting requires patience and persistence, as capturing a single prey often takes significantly more time and effort.

Flexibility

A hunter is very flexible. We see in Jeremiah 16:16, *"And afterward I will send for many hunters, and they shall hunt them from every mountain and every hill, and out of the holes of the rocks."* The hunter can hunt prey in places where a fisherman's boat cannot access.

Diligence

Finally, a good hunter must be diligent. The bible says, *"The lazy man does not roast what he took in hunting, but diligence is man's precious possession."* (Proverbs 12:27) Therefore, a good hunter promptly roasts the prey he catches while hunting. He knows that the prey he caught can start rotting if it is not promptly roasted. Just as roasting a catch is essential for a hunter, following up with a new convert is crucial for a skilled sower. In other words, a skilled sower must be diligent in nurturing and guiding new believers.

Have you ever seen a lion kill prey and then walk away from it? Even in the animal kingdom, they understand that if they do not take their prey away, another animal might swoop in to steal it, or it will begin to rot.

A new convert that is abandoned, i.e. not followed up, is very vulnerable to the enemy's assault. The most critical time for a new believer is the first few days when they give their lives to Jesus Christ. Follow up with your new converts immediately, and ensure they know the next steps to take, now that they are born again.

Fishing

The other way we sow seeds is by being part of a fishing crew. The composition of a fishing crew can range from about two people to an unlimited number of people. When you are part of an enterprise to share the gospel of Jesus Christ, you are fishing with a fishing crew. Jesus told Peter, *"Follow Me, and I will make you fishers of men."* (Matthew 4:19)

Jesus Christ sent out His disciples to go and fish for unbelievers. They went out in pairs to share the gospel.

"After these things, the Lord appointed seventy others also and sent them two by two before His face into every city and place where He Himself was about to go. Then He said to them, 'the harvest truly is great, but the laborers are few; therefore pray to the Lord of the harvest to send out laborers into His harvest field." (Luke 10:1-2)

A fishing expedition can be small-scale or large-scale. It can be mass evangelism (like in Acts 2) or modest expeditions (like that of Paul and Silas). A crusade is an example of fishing. It requires a different set of skills and approach.

When you invite an unbeliever to a church that is passionate about winning souls, you are engaging as part of a fishing crew. Church members invite the people (unbelievers) to church, while the Pastor shares the gospel with them, and invites them to accept Jesus Christ as their Lord and Saviour. In addition, when you financially support an organization, whose purpose is to win souls, you are engaging as part of a fishing crew. Even though you were not the one that invited them to accept Jesus, because you played a role in them being saved, you will receive the same reward as the one who preached the gospel to them and invited them to accept Jesus Christ. This principle is seen in an Old Testament story.

When David and his men had their wives, children and goods taken from them, they eventually got the go-ahead from God to pursue, overtake and recover all that was taken from them. During the pursuit, two hundred of David's men were unable to go ahead, so they were left behind to watch the supplies. After the battle was won, David decided that those who fought the battle would receive the same remuneration as those who waited behind and watched their possessions.

"Now David came to the two hundred men who had been so weary that they could not follow David, whom they also had made to stay at the Brook Besor. So they went out to meet David and to meet the people who were with him. And when David came near the people, he greeted them. Then all the wicked and worthless men of those who went with David answered and said, "Because they did not go with us, we will not give them any of the spoil that we have recovered, except for every man's wife and children, that they may lead them away and depart." But David said, "My brethren, you shall not do so with what the Lord has given us, who has preserved us and delivered into our hand the troop that came against us. For who will heed you in this matter? But as his part is who goes down to the battle, so shall his part be who stays by the supplies; they shall share alike." So it was, from that day

forward; he made it a statute and an ordinance for Israel to this day." (1 Samuel 30:21-25)

Not everyone will be able to physically join a large soul-winning enterprise, but we can all be a part of it by supporting with our resources. Peter was not the one preaching the message on the shore of Lake Gennesaret, but he made his boat available for Jesus to use (Luke 5:1-11). After Jesus was done preaching, it was time to reward those who supported His efforts (Luke 5:4-6). Just like the laws of many nations have provisions to punish accessories to murder, theft, etc., God recognizes and blesses those that contributed to the success of a soul-winning endeavour.

For example, since Cornerstone Christian Church of God (CCCG) financially supports other soul-winning organizations like Christ For All Nations (Reinhard Bonnke Ministries), every financial giver in CCCG will be blessed by God for every soul that Christ For All Nations is winning to Christ all over the world.

A fishing crew must have certain characteristics in order to be successful. We will briefly explore some of those characteristics.

Characteristics of an Effective Fisher

Humility

One of the most vital characteristics a fishing crew must have, to be successful, is humility. Humility is what enables the team to work together. The Bible tells us, *"Submit yourselves to one another in the fear of God."* (Ephesians 5:21)

Because this type of sowing is a joint effort, the team members must be humble for the team to be cohesive. In order for the crew members to submit to their leader, they have to be humble. Anything with more than one head is a monster. For a fishing crew to be successful, there has to be a leader. Note however, that the members of the fishing crew are expected to already be fully convinced their leader is called and empowered by God. Once they are convinced, they should submit to the authority of the leader, in order for the fishing expedition to be successful. The leader should also ensure that every member of the fishing crew that will be directly involved in the sowing is chosen by God.

Humility also extends to the leader, as he/she will have to be able to receive advice from the crew members in their own areas of expertise. Even Jesus Christ was humble enough to ask His disciples for advice on how to feed the multitude. I believe that if they had given a sound suggestion, He would have obliged (John 6:5). The fact that you are leading the fishing crew does not mean you cannot ask your crew members for insight. However, the ultimate decision rests with the leader.

Team Work

The fishing crew has to be able to work together as a team. Just like a healthy human body, every member of the fishing crew must know the role that they play in the team. No one must seek to exalt themselves above the others. An illustration in the Bible paints a perfect picture of a successful fishing crew.

*"Blow the trumpet in Zion, and sound an alarm in My holy mountain! Let all the inhabitants of the land tremble; for the day of the Lord is coming, for it is at hand: a day of darkness and gloominess, a day of clouds and thick darkness, like the morning clouds spread over the mountains. **A people come, great and strong**, the like of whom has never been; nor will there ever be any such after them, even for many successive generations. A fire devours before them, and behind them a flame burns; the land is like the Garden of*

Eden before them, and behind them a desolate wilderness; surely nothing shall escape them. Their appearance is like the appearance of horses; and like swift steeds, so they run. With a noise like chariots over mountaintops they leap, like the noise of a flaming fire that devours the stubble, like a strong people set in battle array. Before them the people writhe in pain; all faces are drained of color. ***They run like mighty men, they climb the wall like men of war; everyone marches in formation, and they do not break ranks. They do not push one another; everyone marches in his own column.*** *Though they lunge between the weapons, they are not cut down. They run to and fro in the city, they run on the wall; they climb into the houses, they enter at the windows like a thief. The earth quakes before them, the heavens tremble; the sun and moon grow dark, and the stars diminish their brightness. The Lord gives voice before His army, for His camp is very great; for strong is the One who executes His word. For the day of the Lord is great and very terrible; who can endure it?"* (Joel 2:1-11)

This passage shows the discipline required for a fishing crew to be effective in evangelism. It is made up of people that know their place. They are good at what they do. They are resilient. They are determined to achieve their stated goals. They are not concerned about self-preservation; instead, their focus is to achieve the goals God has given to the team.

Resourceful

Winning souls through fishing is a resource intensive endeavour. Because a fishing expedition has the potential to haul multitudes into the kingdom of God, lots of resources are needed to successfully execute it.

The resources that are required in a fishing expedition includes financial resources, volunteers, space, materials, equipment, etc. The amount of resources needed for any given fishing expedition is dependent on its size. The larger the size of a fishing expedition, the larger the amount of resources required (and vice versa).

Those that lead a fishing expedition are usually called by God to be Evangelists. An Evangelist has the anointing of God to command forth the resources that will be needed to carry out the task. They are also gifted by God to provide leadership to the team. Because this kind of work can be physically demanding, God has endued Evangelists with unusual strength to carry out this task.

Dependence on God

I have come across countless people who have received a marching order from God to complete an assignment, only to run off on their own to implement it, without allowing God to lead the way. It seems like many people are trying to say to God, "All I need from you is where you want me to go. Once I get the vision, I can find my way there on my own." This sounds completely silly. No matter your excuse, we must never remain in a position where we are not being led by God.

Many believers have believed the lie that, so long as they are doing something good, they are pleasing God. This is absolutely false. Remember that Jesus Himself said, *"Not everyone that saith unto me, Lord, Lord, shall enter into the kingdom of heaven; but he that doeth the will of my Father which is in heaven. Many will say to me on that day, Lord, Lord, have we not prophesied in thy name? and in thy name have cast out devils? and in thy name done many wonderful works? And then will I profess unto them, I never knew you: depart from me, ye that work iniquity."* (Matthew 7:21-23, KJV)

The Word of God also says, *"For as many as are led by the Spirit of God, they are the sons of God."* (Romans 8:14)

Do not fall for this misconception. Acting on God's behalf, without being expressly commissioned by God to do so, is a misrepresentation. It is wrong and improper. God has commissioned us all to preach the gospel, but He still holds the prerogative to assign different believers to different tasks and harvest fields. You are susceptible to the trap of the devil if you keep doing whatever you feel like doing for God, without God's permission.

Even though God desires everyone to be eventually saved (1 Timothy 2:4), there is a time and season appointed by God for that to take place. Salvation is indeed appointed. An appointment means that there is a schedule. It is written in Acts 13:48, *"Now when the Gentiles heard this, they were glad and glorified the word of the Lord. And as many as had been appointed to eternal life believed."* This means that if we are not careful, we might be ministering to people that God has not appointed to be saved yet.

We are not to evangelize based on emotions, human strategy or our own understanding. Allow God to direct your soul-winning endeavours. In soul winning, there is both the human planning side and the aspect where the Holy Spirit leads. Both work in tandem. Whenever there is self-seeking or a selfish agenda on the part of the soul-winner, it will become difficult, if not impossible for them to be led by the Holy Spirit.

The Necessity of Spirit-Led Evangelism: Lessons from Acts 16

There is an interesting account in Acts 16:6-10 that is worthy of analysis.

Now when they had gone through Phrygia and the region of Galatia, they were forbidden by the Holy Spirit to preach the word in Asia. After they had come to Mysia, they tried to go into Bithynia, but the Spirit did not permit them. So passing by Mysia, they came down to Troas. And a vision appeared to Paul in the night. A man of Macedonia stood and pleaded with him, saying, "Come over to Macedonia and help us." Now after he had seen the vision, immediately we sought to go to Macedonia, concluding that the Lord had called us to preach the gospel to them.

Forbidden to Preach the Word in Asia

Paul and Silas were traveling westward through a territory known in the Bible as Asia. The places they visited are now in the country of modern day Turkey. In chapter 16 verse 6, the writer of the Book of Acts says, *"They passed through*

*the Phrygian and Galatian region, having been forbidden
by the Holy Spirit to speak the word in Asia."* Here, we see
the Holy Spirit at work in changing the plans of Paul and
Silas.

When Luke says that the Spirit had forbidden Paul to
speak the Word in Asia, he implies that Paul wanted to
do so. No doubt, at some point, Paul had made his desire
known to his missionary team. Although Luke does not
mention Ephesus, the chief city of Asia, it seems likely that
Paul wanted to proclaim the gospel there. Ephesus was a
great commercial, religious, and cultural center. However, the Holy Spirit postponed Paul's preaching there. In
God's time, Paul went to Ephesus for ministry. He went
there, near the end of his second missionary journey (Acts
18:19-21), and returned on his third journey.

After Paul and Silas arrived in Mysia, in the northwest
of modern Turkey, they wanted to turn north into the
northern province of Bithynia. Apparently, they had a
strategy they wanted to implement. The northern part of
Bithynia was on the southern coast of the Black Sea. A key
city in this northern province was Nicea. This would be a
great place to take the gospel.

Now, for a second time, the Holy Spirit intervened. The Holy Spirit did not permit the missionary team to go to Bithynia. This was a historic moment in the history of the church. The Holy Spirit turned the attention of Paul and his team to Europe instead of Bithynia. Throughout the Book of Acts, the pivotal moments are described as coming from the Spirit. God's strategy for world evangelism was Europe before Asia.

Within fifteen years, Peter finally took the gospel to Bithynia, according to the salutation of his first epistle (1 Peter 1:1).

Led by the Holy Spirit to Macedonia

When the Holy Spirit leads, we know we are acting in accordance with God's time and purpose. Very often, we may wish to do very good things, but it is not God's time. He alone is the master of all things. He alone knows when to act. He alone knows the circumstances that prevail at any given time. Because of this, we can have full confidence in the guidance of the Spirit.

God speaks to us and leads in a variety of ways. Sometimes God reveals His will through a vision. God spoke to Ananias (Acts 9:10-12) in a vision about Paul and his ministry.

The Lord spoke to Cornelius (Acts 10:3) and Peter (Acts 10:17-19; Acts 11:5) in visions. These visions led to the breakthrough of the gospel among the Gentiles.

At Troas, on the northwestern coast of modern Turkey, the Lord spoke to Paul through a vision (Acts 16:9). In the vision, a man from Macedonia was standing and appealing to Paul to come to Macedonia. This was a powerful and persuasive way for Paul to be called. God not only prevented Paul from preaching in Asia and going to Bithynia, but also gave them positive direction on what to do. He called them to Macedonia, which is a part of Europe.

The missionary team (fishing crew) did not hesitate to respond to the call. Acts 16:10 records, *"Immediately we sought to go into Macedonia, concluding that God had called us to preach the gospel to them."*

What a striking story! Twice in this short story, Paul and his team were supernaturally led by the Holy Spirit. Then, Paul had his vision of the man from Macedonia. All these supernatural experiences kept Paul in harmony with God's plan, to keep going through Asia and on to Europe. Proverbs 16:9 sums it up in saying, *"The mind of man plans his way, But the Lord directs his steps."* As we commit ourselves to the Lord, we know that He will lead us day by day. God's strategy must prevail.

Without the active leading of the Holy Spirit, our well-intentioned soul winning endeavours will be a waste. If you continue regardless, you will risk falling into the trap of satisfying yourself, which will eventually lead to pride.

There is time for everything and God is in control of the times and seasons. According to Ecclesiastes 3:1-2, *"To everything there is a season, a time for every purpose under heaven: A time to be born, and a time to die; a time to plant, and a time to pluck what is planted."*

Whenever we are not in alignment with God's will, the devil will have a field day stealing from us. We are most secure when we are in God's perfect will. The most effective way to remain in command and be fruitful is to be fully under God's authority. When we are aligned with God's will, it is impossible for the devil to take advantage of us, except if it was ordained by God to further His plan. For example, the devil believed he was destroying the ministry of Jesus Christ when he moved the people to crucify Him, but never knew that the death of Jesus Christ on the cross was part of God's plan for redeeming mankind. Another example is in the life of Job. Scripture records that Job's latter end was more blessed than his beginning (Job 42:12).

TAKE ACTION

Before you proceed further into this book, I want you to make a commitment to promptly apply what you have learned so far and what you will additionally learn. To do this, I want you to write down the names of people you will reach out to, with the gospel of Jesus Christ. Make a commitment to put what you have learned so far and what you will additionally learn, to immediate practice and you will not regret doing so.

Name:

_____

Name:

_____

Name:

_____

Name:

_____

Name:

_____

Name:

_____

Name:

_____

Name:

_____

Name:

_____

Name:

_____

Name:

_____

Name:

_____

Name:

_____

Name:

_____

Name:

_____

3

The Sower
Sowed the Word

"Listen! Behold, a sower went out to sow."

——*Mark 4:3*

Jesus Christ starts the parable in Mark 4:3 by saying, *"Listen! Behold, a sower went out to sow."* The first step in soul winning is making a decision to go out to sow. Without sowing, there will be no reaping.

If you stop in verse 3, you might go on to assume that you can sow anything, so long as it will get the attention of the unbeliever. This is not true. Jesus went on to clarify in Mark 4:14 that, *"The sower sows the word."* There are many people that advocate showing acts of love to people, in order to win them to Jesus Christ. This is good, so long as you do not forget to sow the word at some point. Showing love to unbelievers without sowing the word, is you, simply engaging in community service. When showing love to people, keep in mind that, *"Whatever you do in word or deed, do all in the name of the Lord Jesus, giving thanks to God the Father through Him."* (Colossians 3:17) At some point, you have to make it clear that you did all you did in the name of Jesus Christ. At some point, you will have to point them to Jesus Christ for their salvation.

From Scriptures, we see that there are two main types of a word to sow in order to yield a harvest of souls. These can be combined or used in isolation. The first is the written or revealed Word of God, and the second is the word of testimony. These two approaches were used by several New Testament saints to turn the hearts of multitudes back to God.

THE WORD OF GOD

This is when we use the Word of God as the main tool for sharing the gospel message to help an unbeliever to know Jesus Christ and why they need to put their trust in Him. Apostle Paul was a skilled sower; He made a profound statement concerning the use of the Word of God to win souls. In Romans 1:16, he boldly declared, *"For I am not ashamed of the gospel of Christ, for it is the power of God to salvation for everyone who believes, for the Jew first and also for the Greek."* The Word of God carries inherent power to win souls, we just need to activate it by sharing it with unbelievers. The Bible is full of examples where the Word of God was used to directly win souls.

The powerful message that Peter delivered on the day of Pentecost was filled with references to the Old Testament. I have emphasized the sections in Peter's address where he referred to other Bible passages.

1. **Joel 2:28-32**

"But Peter, standing up with the eleven, raised his voice and said to them, "Men of Judea and all who dwell in Jerusalem, let this be known to you, and heed my words. For these are not drunk, as you suppose, since it is only the third hour of the day. **But this is what was spoken by the prophet Joel: 'And it shall come to pass in the last days, says God, That I will pour out of My Spirit on all flesh; Your sons and your daughters shall prophesy, Your young men shall see visions, Your old men shall dream dreams. And on My menservants and on My maidservants I will pour out My Spirit in those days; And they shall prophesy. I will show wonders in heaven above and signs in the earth beneath: Blood**

and fire and vapor of smoke. The sun shall be turned into darkness, And the moon into blood, Before the coming of the great and awesome day of the LORD. And it shall come to pass That whoever calls on the name of the LORD Shall be saved.'

2. Psalms 16:8-11

*"Men of Israel, hear these words: Jesus of Nazareth, a Man attested by God to you by miracles, wonders, and signs which God did through Him in your midst, as you yourselves also know— Him, being delivered by the determined purpose and foreknowledge of God, you have taken by lawless hands, have crucified, and put to death; whom God raised up, having loosed the pains of death, because it was not possible that He should be held by it. **For David says concerning Him: 'I foresaw the LORD always before my face, For He is at my right hand, that I may not be shaken. Therefore my heart rejoiced, and my tongue was glad; Moreover my flesh also will rest in hope. For You will not leave my soul in Hades, Nor will You allow Your Holy One to see corruption. You have made known to me the ways of life; You will make me full of joy in Your presence.'***

3. Psalms 110:1

*"Men and brethren, let me speak freely to you of the pa-triarch David, that he is both dead and buried, and his tomb is with us to this day. Therefore, being a prophet, and knowing that God had sworn with an oath to him that of the fruit of his body, according to the flesh, He would raise up the Christ to sit on his throne, he, foreseeing this, spoke concerning the resurrection of the Christ, that His soul was not left in Hades, nor did His flesh see corruption. This Jesus God has raised up, of which we are all witnesses. Therefore being exalted to the right hand of God, and having received from the Father the promise of the Holy Spirit, He poured out this which you now see and hear. "For David did not ascend into the heavens, **but he says himself: 'The LORD said to my Lord, "Sit at My right hand, till I make Your enemies Your footstool."'***

4. Acts 2:14-41

"Therefore let all the house of Israel know assuredly that God has made this Jesus, whom you crucified, both Lord and Christ." Now when they heard this, they were cut to the heart, and said to Peter and the rest of the apostles, "Men and brethren, what shall we do?" Then Peter said to them, "Repent, and let every one of you be baptised in the name of

Jesus Christ for the remission of sins; and you shall receive the gift of the Holy Spirit. For the promise is to you and to your children, and to all who are afar off, as many as the Lord our God will call." And with many other words he testified and exhorted them, saying, "Be saved from this perverse generation." Then those who gladly received his word were baptized; and that day about three thousand souls were added to them."

From Peter's sermon, you can see that he quoted scriptures and explained them, in an attempt to convince his listeners that Jesus Christ is Lord, and they should put their trust in Him.

You can use this approach when under the unction of the Holy Spirit. You can also use this approach when you have adequately *"Studied to show yourself approved, a worker who does not need to be ashamed, rightly dividing the word of truth."* (2 Timothy 2:15).

Sharing the Word of God with people for the purpose of salvation should not be mistaken for arguing with people on the veracity of the Bible. It should also not be mistaken for finding every opportunity to point out people's sins to them.

An example is seen when the scribes and Pharisees brought a woman caught in adultery to Jesus Christ (John 8:1-12). They said to Jesus, *"Teacher, this woman was caught in adultery, in the very act. Now Moses, in the law, commanded us that such should be stoned. But what do You say?"* (verse 4–5)

These scribes and Pharisees were not concerned with restoring the soul of the adulteress. Instead, they were fixated on judgement. That was why Jesus said, only those without sin should throw a stone at her first.

Throwing a stone is the equivalent of maliciously using the Scriptures to judge others, while deliberately ignoring our own misgivings. When we recognize that we were saved by grace, our approach in sharing the word with others for the purpose of salvation will be that of humility, as one saved by grace, and not one of pride, as one saved by their good deeds.

According to Galatians 5:18, *"If you are led by the Spirit, you are not under the law."* The law, or principle, in this case is to remove the log from your eyes before you attempt to remove the speck from another's. This admonition is found in Mark 7:3-5, *"And why do you look at the speck in your brother's eye, but do not consider the plank in your own eye? Or how can you say to your brother, 'Let me remove the speck from your eye'; and look, a plank is in your own eye? Hypocrite! First remove the plank from your own eye, and then you will see clearly to remove the speck from your brother's eye."* Going by this principle, perhaps only a handful of believers should preach the word to an unbeliever. However, when we are led by the Holy Spirit in sharing the word, our own misgivings do not matter.

It's high time we believers understood that God's desire is for many people to escape the judgment of sin. God's purpose is not to destroy as many humans as possible, but to save as many humans as possible. 1 Timothy 2:3-4 confirms that we ought to pray for all men, *"For this is good and acceptable in the sight of God our Savior, who desires all men to be saved and to come to the knowledge of the truth."*

One of the main challenges that Christians face is the fear that even though they strongly desire to tell unbelievers about Jesus Christ, they do not know enough scriptures to do so. As a result, they wait to learn more scriptures before they are comfortable enough to share the gospel with those that are perishing. This is not ideal. Many people are perishing, and delay can be very costly. Praise God, for there is a way of escape for people that are in this category. It is winning souls by sharing testimonies.

The Word of Testimony

The Bible tells us that, *"They overcame him by the blood of the Lamb and by the word of their testimony."* (Revelation 12:11) Sharing your testimonies or that of others is an effective way to tell others about Jesus Christ—by sharing His acts in people's lives.

A testimony is a proof that Jesus Christ is alive, and He is the Saviour. What has Jesus Christ done for you? Were you blind but now you can see? Were you bound by fear but now you are free to live? Do you know someone that Jesus Christ has performed a miracle of healing on? Was there a marriage that was heading for the rocks that Jesus Christ restored? These and many more, are tools in your arsenal for sharing the gospel.

Everyone alive is looking for one thing or the other. Sadly, many of those people go to the devil for things that Jesus Christ freely gives. By sharing testimonies with others, you are boosting their faith as you make them aware of what is available in Jesus Christ.

When you tell an unbeliever that is sick in the hospital that Jesus Christ is the healer, and you share a testimony of healing with them, you are sowing the word in their heart.

At the time of writing this book, an event took place that is relevant to the theme of this book. A certain member of Cornerstone Christian Church of God was going to share the gospel with a sick relative in another city. He came to me asking for tips that can help him effectively share the gospel with that relative. I simply told him to arm himself with three scriptures and some testimonies of healing that he was familiar with. At the time of writing this book, he had shared the gospel with that relative and even prayed over the relative to be healed. It is my joy to report that the relative accepted Jesus Christ, before going to be with the Lord.

Testimonies are so powerful that they are also heavily used by marketing professionals and organizations selling products or rendering services. They are usually called testimonials or reviews. The objective testimonials/reviews from others give us more confidence in the product/service being advertised.

The Word of Testimony in Scripture

The Samaritan Woman

We see a powerful example of the use of testimonies, in John 4, to effectively sharing the gospel with others. This story is about the Samaritan woman's encounter with Jesus Christ. Jesus Christ corrected her understanding of worship and even told her how many husbands she had prior to her current man-friend with benefits. This Samaritan woman single-handedly won many in the city to Christ. Did she achieve this by memorizing and regurgitating the whole Bible or by memorizing and regurgitating Billy Graham's message? No, absolutely not! She achieved this feat by passionately sharing her testimony with others in the city. In John 4:39 we are told that, *"And many of the Samaritans of that city believed in Him because of the word of the woman who testified, 'He told me all that I ever did.'"* (John 4:39)

This woman is perhaps the only person in the Bible that made the best use of her encounter with Jesus Christ. Think on this, even those raised from the dead did not win as many souls to Christ with their testimony as this Samaritan woman. The truth is that she could have decided to despise the fact that Jesus only told her what happened in her past and her liaisons with men. Instead, she was very grateful and made a big deal of it. She did not care that in sharing her testimony she might have to tell the people that Jesus knew she had been with several men.

I know people that have received significant miracles from God but are too self-conscious to share with others. They have been healed, delivered, provided for, protected, etc. but are either too self-conscious to share it with others, or despise their testimonies. To despise your testimony means to think that it is not significant enough to share with others. This is a gross error. Every good gift you have received is from above (James 1:17) and must be acknowledged as such.

The Demon-Possessed Man of Gadara

There was another man in Mark 5 that was demon-possessed. He was possessed by a legion of demons. The demons made him stay in the mountains and in tombs, crying out and cutting himself with stones. When the people in that city saw that Jesus delivered the man from the demons, they were afraid of Him and asked Him to leave their city. Mark 5:18, however, narrates that, *"When He got into the boat, he who had been demon-possessed begged Him that he might be with Him."* This man wanted to leave with Jesus Christ.

At this point, you might have expected Jesus to allow the man to follow Him everywhere as a disciple. You might also have expected Christ to tell the man to study the Word of God, so he can preach to the entire city. Instead, Jesus gave him a simple instruction.

However, Jesus did not permit him, but said to him, "Go home to your friends, and tell them what great things the Lord has done for you, and how He has had compassion on you." And he departed and began to proclaim in Decapolis all that Jesus had done for him; and all marvelled." (Mark 5:19-20)

A testimony from the mouth of the recipient or someone that witnessed it firsthand is a very powerful tool for winning people to Jesus Christ. Note that in Mark 5:20, the people marvelled. This means that the testimony they heard from the formerly madman resonated with them.

Begin to cultivate the practice of sharing your testimonies with people. Every opportunity you have, tell someone what Jesus Christ has done for you. It is much better than gossiping about other people. It is much better than talking about the weather. I encourage you to start sharing your testimony with others today. By doing so, you will be helping to spread the good news of the Kingdom of God.

God, Himself declared that King David was a man after His own heart. This is evident in the fact that he made it his duty to declare the mighty works of God. David declared the righteous acts and salvation of God on a daily basis. Will you make it your duty today to declare God's mighty works to everyone that cares to listen? God bless you as you do so.

"My mouth shall tell of Your righteousness And Your salvation all the day, For I do not know their limits. I will go in the strength of the Lord GOD; I will make mention of Your righteousness, of Yours only. O God, You have taught me from my youth; And to this day I declare Your wondrous works." (Psalms 71:15-17)

4

Some Fell by the Wayside

"And it happened, as he sowed, that some seed fell by the wayside; and the birds of the air came and devoured it."

——*Mark 4:4*

Every good seed has a natural ability to bear fruit. The problem, however, is that the quality of the seed is inconsequential if it is not sown in a good soil. The word (testimonies and the Scriptures) is a good seed and it is potent in fruit bearing. However, when it is exposed to an enemy that is keen on stealing it, the word might not bear fruit. Every word that is sown has the inherent ability to bear fruit in the heart of the hearer.

THE BATTLE FOR THE SEED

Birds of the Air

While explaining the parable of the sower in Mark 4:14, Jesus revealed the identity of the *"birds of the air"* as Satan. You might be wondering why He referred to Satan in the plural form—birds. The reason is that Satan fulfills this mission of stealing the word we hear through his numerous principalities, powers, rulers of darkness in high places and demons. This thought is further echoed in 2 Corinthians 4:3-4, *"But even if our gospel is veiled, it is veiled to those who are perishing, whose minds the god of this age has blinded, who do not believe, lest the light of the gospel of the glory of Christ, who is the image of God, should shine on them."*

As a sower, you must be fully aware that the devil will not allow any seed sown to bear fruit. If every Word of God we heard was allowed to bear fruit, our level of spiritual growth will be phenomenal. Most of the seeds sown in people's hearts are taken away before they leave the parking lot. The devil and his cohorts mount coordinated assaults on the hearts of the hearers of the word, in order to cause the word they are hearing to be unfruitful.

Every unbeliever is under the influence of the devil. Every unbeliever is in the kingdom of darkness, which is ruled over by the devil. Going to sow seeds in the hearts of people, under the dominion of darkness, without first and foremost taking authority over the owner of that kingdom, will lead to frustration.

The sower that will have their seed successfully penetrate the hearts of their hearers must take authority over these seed-thieves. These seed-thieves must be bound and their influence over those we are speaking to must be curtailed. Jesus said in Mark 3:26-27, *"And if Satan has risen up against himself, and is divided, he cannot stand, but has an end. No one can enter a strong man's house and plunder his goods, unless he first binds the strong man. And then he will plunder his house."*

As a sower, you must learn how to conduct spiritual warfare before engaging in seed-sowing. We must prayerfully prepare before reaching out to people with the gospel.

Combating the Birds of the Air

A skilled sower must also be skilled in spiritual warfare.

Spiritual warfare is the art of engaging with forces of darkness. Even though children of God are already assured victory in every spiritual warfare, we must be skilled to know how to engage the enemy to gain victory.

In spiritual warfare, ignorance is one of the most lethal weapons. We are told not to be ignorant of the devices of the enemy (2 Corinthians 2:11). The devil thrives under the cloak of darkness. This is why a skilled sower must not live by sight, i.e. only believe what they see, feel, hear, touch or smell. Their awareness and response to spiritual things must not be based on physical senses.

Also, a skilled sower must be aware of the weapons at their disposal in waging spiritual warfare, before going out to sow seeds. Note that the pieces of armour listed out in scripture (Ephesians 6) is not to be declared before spiritual warfare. I have heard believers pray prayers like, "I gird my waist with truth" or "I put on the helmet of salvation," etc. If you do not live your life based on the truth of God's word or if you are not saved, it is a waste of time to declare these things before spiritual warfare. We never saw any of the New Testament believers do this. The demons recognised Paul the Apostle (Acts 19:15) because all the pieces of the armour in Ephesians 6 was worn as part of his daily life.

Let us examine the individual pieces of the whole armor of God found in Ephesians 6:10-18.

"Finally, my brethren, be strong in the Lord and in the power of His might. Put on the whole armor of God, that you may be able to stand against the wiles of the devil. For we do not wrestle against flesh and blood, but against principalities, against powers, against the rulers of the darkness of this age, against spiritual hosts of wickedness in the heavenly places. Therefore take up the whole armor of God, that you may be able to withstand in the evil day, and having done all, to stand. Stand therefore, having girded your waist with truth, having put on the breastplate of righteousness, and having shod your feet with the preparation of the gospel of peace; above all, taking the shield of faith with which you will be able to quench all the fiery darts of the wicked one. And take the helmet of salvation, and the sword of the Spirit, which is the word of God; praying always with all prayer and supplication in the Spirit, being watchful to this end with all perseverance and supplication for all the saints."

The Armour of Christ

Truth

"Stand therefore, having girded your waist with truth." (Ephesians 6:14)

The first piece of armour that Paul stated is, girding your waist with truth.

Spiritual warfare is waged with the truth. Jesus Christ is the way, the truth and the life (John 14:6). Jesus Christ also said, *"Sanctify them by Your truth. Your word is truth."* (John 17:17) The truth is something we live our lives by. Girding our waist with truth ensures that every other aspect of our lives does not get out of order. It keeps us from being exposed and hides our private parts from public view. When you gird your waist with truth, you are protecting yourself from the enemy discovering the inner workings of your life.

What does it mean to live your life based on the truth of God's word? To live your life based on the truth of God's word is to follow the instructions you receive from the written or revealed word of God. It means that you are not led by your opinion, public opinion or satanic opinion, but by what God's word says. It means that you choose to forgive a person that hurt you, just because the Word of God says so. This is what it means to gird your waist with truth. Failure to gird your waist with truth will expose you to the devil's attacks.

Breastplate of Righteousness

"Having put on the breastplate of righteousness." (Ephesians 6:14)

The breastplate covers the heart. The breastplate of righteousness is the consciousness a skilled sower has that they are righteous. Righteousness means being right with God. The worst time to doubt your righteousness is when you are engaging in spiritual warfare. I will share a story with you that illustrates this truth.

Before Cornerstone Christian Church of God was founded, I was part of a local church in Edmonton, Alberta. While the pastor was preaching during a particular service, the demon in a woman sitting at the back of the church began to manifest. She began to scream and jerk erratically. As you can imagine, this captured the attention of the congregation. While we were all thinking about what to do, a gentleman, who was seated close to her, stood up with boldness to rebuke the demon in the woman. Immediately the gentleman stood before the woman, the demon screamed loudly, "How dare you come here? Do you think I don't know what you do?" Immediately the demon said this, the man turned around and walked out of the church with his tail between his legs. At that time, the gentleman was an adulterer and fornicator, and the demon knew this. You can deceive human beings, but you cannot deceive spirit beings. Things are visible in the spirit realm.

To effectively wage spiritual warfare, you must be in right standing with God. This does not mean that you do not make mistakes, but that you genuinely repent of them immediately you are convicted.

Preparation of the Gospel of Peace

"And having shod your feet with the preparation of the gospel of peace." (Ephesians 6:15)

In spiritual warfare, we prepare our feet by being on the go for God in spreading the good news of the kingdom of God. The feet of people that share the good news of the kingdom of God are beautiful. The gospel is the good news of God's plan of redemption.

How beautiful upon the mountains are the feet of him who brings good news, who proclaims peace, who brings glad tidings of good things, who proclaims salvation, who says to Zion, "Your God reigns!" (Isaiah 52:7)

Notice that Ephesians 6:15 says, *"With the preparation of the gospel of peace."* The moment you make up your mind to be enlisted among the number of those that share the gospel and prepare accordingly, your feet are protected. Reading this book is a demonstration of your desire to share the gospel.

Shield of Faith

"Above all, taking the shield of faith with which you will be able to quench all the fiery darts of the wicked one." (Ephesians 5:16)

Faith is not only needed for pleasing God (Hebrews 11:6) or doing the supernatural (Mark 11:23). Faith is also actively used in spiritual warfare.

The devil throws fiery darts at believers during spiritual warfare. During that moment, faith is needed to overcome it. In the course of spiritual warfare, the devil will lob accusations at you. He will suggest outlandish thoughts to you. He will suggest that God is not pleased with you. He might even dare say that you are not empowered enough to be victorious. Perhaps he will say that you have not fasted and prayed enough to be able to overcome spiritual battles. Your faith in God's word concerning that situation is what will keep you going. During that time of spiritual warfare, it will seem like what the devil is saying is true. Without faith, you will give in to the devil's suggestions and be defeated.

Faith comes by hearing, and hearing by the Word of God (Romans 10:17). The more you connect with the Word of God with an open heart, the more your faith grows. You will never be victorious in spiritual warfare if you do not spend time in the Word of God. We see in Corinthians 3:18: *"But we all, with unveiled face, beholding as in a mirror the glory of the Lord, are being transformed into the same image from glory to glory, just as by the Spirit of the Lord."* Approach God through His word with an "unveiled face" in order to be transformed from glory to glory. Unveiled face simply means to be vulnerable, to have no hidden agenda, to have no preconceived notions, to be open to correction, and to come with a sincere heart.

Helmet of Salvation

"And take the helmet of salvation." (Ephesians 6:17)

In order to wage spiritual warfare, you must be saved. Without being saved, you are under the sway of the devil and cannot fight the devil. A kingdom divided against itself cannot stand (Mark 3:24). You must fulfil the conditions of salvation to be saved. The conditions are simple. You must confess with your mouth the Lord Jesus and believe in your heart that God has raised Him from the dead. Do you see why the devil is attacking the truth that Jesus Christ was raised from the dead? This is critical to our salvation.

"But what does it say? "The word is near you, in your mouth and in your heart" (that is, the word of faith which we preach): that if you confess with your mouth the Lord Jesus and believe in your heart that God has raised Him from the dead, you will be saved. For with the heart, one believes unto righteousness, and with the mouth, confession is made unto salvation. For the Scripture says, "Whoever believes on Him will not be put to shame." For there is no distinction between Jew and Greek, for the same Lord over all is rich to all who call upon Him. For "whoever calls on the name of the Lord shall be saved." (Romans 10:8-13)

Have you confessed with your mouth that Jesus Christ is Lord? Do you believe in your heart that God has raised Jesus from the dead? If you are unsure of your salvation, please repair your spiritual foundation today. If you have difficulty believing that Jesus Christ was raised from the dead, read any of the Bible accounts about it (i.e. Matthew, Mark, Luke and John). Immediately skip to the section of this book with the sinner's prayer and say it with all your heart.

Sword of the Spirit

"And the sword of the Spirit, which is the word of God." (Ephesians 6:17)

The Word of God is the sword of the Spirit. It is the only offensive weapon in the whole armour of God. It is the only offensive weapon recognized in the spirit realm. The Word of God cannot be used offensively unless it is spoken in faith.

In Luke 4, we see that Jesus Christ Himself used the word when He encountered the devil in combat. Jesus Christ thrust the sword of the Spirit on the side of Satan three times simply by saying *"It is written."* By the third unsuccessful attempt to defeat Jesus Christ, the devil left Him until an opportune time.

But Jesus answered him, saying, "It is written, 'Man shall not live by bread alone, but by every word of God.'" (Luke 4:4)

And Jesus answered and said to him, "Get behind Me, Satan! For it is written, 'You shall worship the Lord your God, and Him only you shall serve.'" (Luke 4:8)

And Jesus answered and said to him, "It has been said, 'You shall not tempt the Lord your God.'" (Luke 4:12)

A closed mouth is a closed destiny. It is important to engage the enemy with the power of the spoken word.

Before ascending to the right-hand side of the Father, Jesus Christ advised His disciples in this manner: *"But when they arrest you and deliver you up, do not worry beforehand, or premeditate what you will speak. But whatever is given you in that hour, speak that; for it is not you who speak, but the Holy Spirit."* (Mark 13:11)

This same principle applies when we are engaging in spiritual warfare. If your heart is filled with the Word of God, the Holy Spirit will draw out what is needed for each battle. Ensure you are regularly meditating on the Word of God; leave the rest to Him in time of battle.

Praying in the Spirit

"Praying always with all prayer and supplication in the Spirit." (Ephesians 6:18)

No matter how spiritual you are, we can never know as much as God knows. The Holy Spirit is God and He is dwelling in the hearts of believers to help us succeed in life. The Holy Spirit is also our helper when it comes to spiritual warfare. When we have exhausted our vocabularies in prayer, we must remember that we have a spiritual warfare helper in the person of the Holy Spirit. Read what the Bible says about this: *"For we do not know what we should pray for as we ought, but the Spirit Himself makes intercession for us with groanings which cannot be uttered. Now He who searches the hearts knows what the mind of the Spirit is, because He makes intercession for the saints according to the will of God."* (Romans 8:26-27)

Praying in the Spirit causes confusion in the camp of the enemy because they do not understand what we are saying. This is so because when we pray in the Spirit, we are speaking mysteries (1 Corinthians 14:2). You are not understood, but your effect can be seen and felt.

"The wind blows where it wishes, and you hear the sound of it, but cannot tell where it comes from and where it goes. So is everyone who is born of the Spirit." (John 3:8)

Praying in the Spirit also builds up the faith of a believer. We are told in Jude 1:20, *"But you, beloved, building yourselves up on your most holy faith, praying in the Holy Spirit."* Praying in the Spirit is to the spirit of man, what lifting weights is to the body. The longer you pray in the Spirit, the stronger your spirit becomes. The stronger your spirit is, the more equipped you are to defeat the enemy in spiritual warfare. Remember, *"If thou faint in the day of adversity, your strength is small."* (Proverbs 24:10)

Strength can be measured in two ways: endurance and force. Endurance is measured by how long you can persevere before giving up, while force is measured by the impact from your strength. Some believers have one or the other. It is imperative that you have both endurance and force. We use both types of strength in spiritual warfare. Sometimes, the battle is protracted but not too forceful. At other times, however, the battle is considerably forceful but ephemeral. Praying in the Spirit will help you build both types of strength.

Be Watchful

"Being watchful to this end with all perseverance and supplication for all the saints." (Ephesians 6:18)

It is important that we are sensitive to what is going on around us. The Bible tells us: *"But while men slept, his enemy came and sowed tares among the wheat and went his way"* (Matthew 13:25). It takes spiritual sensitivity to engage the enemy. Be watchful of suggestions he brings to your mind. Be watchful of the influences he might send your way to detract from you. The cunning nature of the enemy can enable him to evade detection. We thank God that we can see, hear and perceive spiritually. The Bible again warns us thus: *"Watch and pray, lest you enter into temptation. The spirit indeed is willing, but the flesh is weak"* (Matthew 26:41).

Being watchful is not the same as being fearful, anxious or worrisome. As believers, we are not meant to be fearful, neither are we to be anxious nor worrisome. Being watchful is to enjoy the fellowship of the Holy Spirit and display His fruit in our lives, while being observant. For example, you could be expecting a guest but still be reading a book at the same time. You do not necessarily have to stand at the door, glancing at everyone passing by. If you are confident that your guest will arrive, you can carry on with other activities while still paying attention to the door buzzer.

If you have the tendency to easily get distracted, pray and ask God to help you. To be effective in spiritual warfare, you must be watchful. Say this prayer:

"Heavenly Father, I come to you today asking that you perfect me. Enable me to watch and pray. Help me to be sensitive to what is happening in and around me in Jesus' name I pray. Amen!"

We Wrestle NOT Against Flesh and Blood

When dealing with an unbeliever, it is very important to recognize that their actions or inactions are dictated by the devil and his minions. Do not take things personally, or else you will be bruised, broken and beaten. Recognize that, it is the devil in that unbeliever that is making them curse you out when you are sharing the gospel with them.

Be Strong

We are told to be strong in the Lord. We must engage in spiritual warfare from a place of strength and confidence, instead of fear and trembling. Fear can be easily spotted in the spiritual realm. Let the weak say I am strong (Joel 3:10). He who is in you is greater than he that is in the world (1 John 4:4).

5

Some Fell on Stony Ground

"Some fell on stony ground, where it did not have much earth; and immediately it sprang up because it had no depth of earth. But when the sun was up it was scorched, and because it had no root it withered away."

——*Luke 4:5-6*

In explaining the category of seeds that fell on stony ground, Jesus said: *"These likewise are the ones sown on stony ground who, when they hear the word, immediately receive it with gladness; and they have no root in themselves, and so endure only for a time. Afterward, when tribulation or persecution arises for the word's sake, immediately they stumble."* (Luke 4:16-17)

Have you ever experienced this when preaching to people? When you initially preach to them, they are excited, and they say the sinner's prayer, but afterward, they are nowhere to be found. In some cases, they avoid you like a plague. This is the category Jesus is speaking about here. Is it possible to help people in this category? The answer is yes. A skilled sower knows the seeds that will need a different condition in order to thrive. A skilled sower knows that not everyone who excitedly receives the gospel is going to last in the faith, unless we identify them and do something to help them.

A skilled sower travails in prayers for unbelievers to know Jesus Christ. We should also travail in prayers, in order for Christ to be formed in them. That is why Paul said in Galatians 4:19, *"My little children, for whom I labour in birth again until Christ is formed in you."* We cannot simply abandon the people who gladly received the Word of God we have sown in their hearts. What then should be done? We must help them to gain root. If the problem is that they have no root in themselves, it is our responsibility to help them gain root. Apostle Paul corroborates this in Colossians 2:7, *"Rooted and built up in Him and established in the faith, as you have been taught, abounding in it with thanksgiving."* We will examine some ways, other than prayer, to help unbelievers gain root so they can be established in the faith.

SUPPORTING UNBELIEVERS IN TAKING ROOT

Imagine this scenario. You see a woman that has carried a baby to term. She has endured nine grueling months and it is finally time to deliver her baby girl. Her bag is packed up and she is taken to the hospital in expectation of the delivery. As she announces that her water just broke, she is immediately rushed to the delivery room. Her husband is by her side and dutifully encourages her to push. She screams while holding her husband's hands and finally the baby is here. Everyone in the delivery room heaves a euphoric sigh of relief. Joy and excitement replace the pressure that was initially in the delivery room, as the baby is handed over to her mother. The mother adores her newborn baby; she takes a selfie and posts it online for the entire world to see. The mother then places this bundle of joy on the bed next to her, and announces to the doctor and nurses that it is time for her to go home. To the amazement of the doctor and nurses, she exits the hospital with her husband by her side but leaves the child behind.

Is there something wrong with this scenario? Absolutely there is. This is what many well-meaning Christians do when they lead unbelievers to Jesus Christ. Once the unbeliever says the sinner's prayer, they are abandoned, and we wonder what happened to them. We wonder why they are not automatically living a triumphant Christian life like everyone else. We wonder why they are not diligently attending church services and joining service groups.

There is a reason why God made sure that children are born into a family where they are nurtured to grow. If God used you as a vessel in getting a person saved, you immediately bear the responsibility of a spiritual parent to that person. It becomes your responsibility to ensure that the next steps are followed, after giving their lives to Jesus Christ.

It is the duty of a spiritual parent to follow up with new-converts immediately after their conversion. This is the time when they are the most vulnerable. They will have many questions that they need answers to. The devil will work overtime to make them doubt their salvation and backslide. If that happens, it will become way more difficult for them to come back to Jesus Christ.

Request for the contact information of your new converts. Get as much information from them as they are willing to share. This will enable you to contact them to inquire about their welfare.

Immediately they give their hearts to Jesus Christ, you want to make sure that they join a community of believers. This was how the early church in the book of Acts kept most of the souls that they were given by God. To get more details on what to do, immediately after an unbeliever has been won to Jesus Christ, please read my book titled: "Now That You Are Born Again, What Next?"

*And with many other words he testified and exhorted them, saying, "Be saved from this perverse generation." Then those who gladly received his word were baptized; and that day about three thousand souls were added to them. **And they continued steadfastly in the apostles' doctrine and fellowship, in the breaking of bread, and in prayers.** Then fear came upon every soul, and many wonders and signs were done through the apostles. **Now all who believed were together,** and had all things in common, and sold their possessions and goods, and divided them among all, as anyone had need. **So continuing daily with one accord in the temple, and breaking bread from house to house,** they ate their food with gladness and simplicity of* *heart, praising God and having favor with all the people. And the Lord added to the church daily those who were being saved."* (Acts 2:40-47)

Do you see from the passage above that the early church did not just win souls and leave them to grow by themselves? They were actively involved in ensuring that the new converts were established in the faith and grew roots in themselves.

The support from like-minded believers, is the moisture that was lacking in the heart of those whose seed was quickly taken away from them, because of the absence of roots. Encourage your new-converts. Remind them of the love of God. Demonstrate to them that even though they made a mistake, so long as they come to God in penitence, they will not be tossed out by God.

Milk of the Word of God

Just like newborn babies, a new convert needs the pure milk of the word to grow. This is not the time to engage them in spiritual warfare. Baby Jesus was powerless to save Himself from Herod and had to be whisked away to Egypt for His safety.

New converts need to understand the basic doctrines of the Word of God, e.g. the reality of their salvation, their new nature, the love of their Heavenly Father, etc. Scripture tells us that *"As newborn babes, desire the pure milk of the word, that you may grow thereby."* (1 Peter 2:2) Apostle Paul also alluded in 1 Corinthians 3:2, *"I fed you with milk and not with solid food; for until now you were not able to receive it, and even now you are still not able."*

Teach your new converts how to read the Bible. Encourage them to start reading the Bible from the New Testament, especially the gospels. They need to immediately get acquainted with their Lord and Saviour, Jesus Christ. Perhaps one of the reasons why many Christians fail to understand the love of God is that they started reading the Bible from the Old Testament, and hence got acquainted with the Father in the Old Testament.

Baptism of the Holy Spirit

Jesus introduced the Holy Spirit to His disciples before He departed from them. He promised: *"And I will pray the Father, and He will give you another Helper, that He may abide with you forever—the Spirit of truth, whom the world cannot receive, because it neither sees Him nor knows Him;*

but you know Him, for He dwells with you and will be in you." (John 14:16-17)

On one occasion, he gave them this command in Acts 1:4-5 (NIV): *"Do not leave Jerusalem, but wait for the gift my Father promised **(in John 14:16-17)**, which you have heard me speak about. For John baptized with water, but in a few days you will be baptized with the Holy Spirit."*

The promise was fulfilled when the Holy Spirit descended on the thirsty disciples, now Apostles, as they heeded Christ's instructions to tarry in Jerusalem until that promise was fulfilled.

"When the day of Pentecost came, they were all together in one place. Suddenly a sound like the blowing of a violent wind came from heaven and filled the whole house where they were sitting. They saw what seemed to be tongues of fire that separated and came to rest on each of them. All of them were filled with the Holy Spirit and began to speak in other tongues as the Spirit enabled them." (Acts 2:1-4)

Baptism simply means an immersion. Baptism in the Holy Spirit means being filled with the Holy Spirit. This should not be mistaken with being born again. We become born again when we accept that Jesus is Lord. However, from the account in Acts 10, we see that being baptized in the

Holy Spirit can happen at the same time as being born again.

Cornelius

We saw this happen in the story of Cornelius.

"There was a certain man in Caesarea called Cornelius, a centurion of what was called the Italian Regiment, a devout man and one who feared God with all his household, who gave alms generously to the people, and prayed to God always. About the ninth hour of the day he saw clearly in a vision an angel of God coming in and saying to him, "Cornelius!" And when he observed him, he was afraid, and said, "What is it, lord?" So he said to him, "Your prayers and your alms have come up for a memorial before God. Now send men to Joppa, and send for Simon whose surname is Peter. He is lodging with Simon, a tanner, whose house is by the sea. He will tell you what you must do." (Acts 10:1-6)

Even though Cornelius was devout, he was not born again, because he had not heard the gospel of Christ or had the chance to accept Jesus Christ into his heart. The Lord then sent an angel to ask Cornelius to send for Peter. Peter's mission was to preach the gospel to Cornelius and his household, so they can believe in Jesus Christ. We are told in Acts 10:44-46 that, *"While Peter was still speaking these words, the Holy Spirit fell upon all those who heard the word. And those of the circumcision who believed were astonished, as many as came with Peter, because the gift of the Holy Spirit had been poured out on the Gentiles also. For they heard them speak with tongues and magnify God."*

The word **"heard "** in verse 44 means that, they received the word that Peter spoke concerning Jesus as the Christ. Once that happened, according to John 1:12, they became children of God; thereby, fulfilling the condition to receive the baptism of the Holy Spirit.

The Disciples

In many other instances in Scriptures, including that of the disciples, the people became born again before receiving the baptism of the Holy Spirit. This passage shows that the disciples received Jesus as the Christ and Lord while He was still with them.

"Then, the same day at evening, being the first day of the week, when the doors were shut where the disciples were assembled, for fear of the Jews, Jesus came and stood in the midst, and said to them, "Peace be with you." When He had said this, He showed them His hands and His side. Then the

disciples were glad when they saw the Lord. So Jesus said to them again, "Peace to you! As the Father has sent Me, I also send you." And when He had said this, He breathed on them, and said to them, "Receive the Holy Spirit. If you forgive the sins of any, they are forgiven them; if you retain the sins of any, they are retained." (John 20:19-23)

It was not until Acts 2:1-4 that the Apostles received the baptism of the Holy Spirit.

The Early Converts

Another example in Scripture is of the early converts, who received Jesus as Lord before being subsequently baptized in the Holy Spirit.

Then Peter said to them, "Repent, and let every one of you be baptized in the name of Jesus Christ for the remission of sins; and you shall receive the gift of the Holy Spirit. For the promise is to you and to your children, and to all who are afar off, as many as the Lord our God will call." And with many other words he testified and exhorted them, saying, "Be saved from this perverse generation." Then those who gladly received his word were baptised; and that day about three thousand souls were added to them." (Acts 2:38-41)

The Samaritans

The Samaritans in Acts 8 are another example. Acts 8:4-6, shows the people in Samaria accepting Jesus as Lord: *"Therefore those who were scattered went everywhere preaching the word. Then Philip went down to the city of Samaria and preached Christ to them. And the multitudes with one accord heeded the things spoken by Philip, hearing and seeing the miracles which he did."*

Subsequently, in Acts 8:14-17, we see the believers in Samaria receiving the baptism of the Holy Spirit: *"Now when the apostles who were at Jerusalem heard that Samaria had received the word of God, they sent Peter and John to them, who, when they had come down, prayed for them that they might receive the Holy Spirit. For as yet He had fallen upon none of them. They had only been baptized in the name of the Lord Jesus. Then they laid hands on them, and they received the Holy Spirit."*

We have established that being born again and being baptized in the Holy Spirit are two distinct and separate experiences, even though they could happen at the same time. The early church always made sure that new converts were baptized in the Holy Spirit.

A new convert's root is established when we follow the principles the early church followed.

6

Some Fell on Thorns

"And some seed fell among thorns; and the thorns grew up and choked it, and it yielded no crop."

——*Mark 4:7*

A skilled sower must watch out for seeds that will fall on thorns. Jesus explained this category in Mark 4:18-19: *"Now these are the ones sown among thorns; they are the ones who hear the word, and the cares of this world, the deceitfulness of riches, and the desires for other things entering in choke the word, and it becomes unfruitful."*

Can people in this category be rescued? The answer is yes. If Jesus Christ was able to rescue humanity and restore us back to God, by dying on the cross, then truly all things are possible to him who believes (Mark 9:23).

The parable of the prodigal son (Luke 15:11-32) vividly paints the picture of the plausibility of rescuing people that fall for the cares of this world, the deceitfulness of riches and the desires for other things.

Every well-meaning child of God will be tempted. We will all have our faith tested. Some will pass, while some might fail. Some will repent and be restored, while some will not. The aim of this section is to help reduce the number of believers whose seeds will fall among the thorns.

GOOD TREE VS. BAD TREE

In teaching us how to identify false prophets, Jesus gave us insight into good trees and bad trees. Jesus said, *"You will know them by their fruits. Do men gather grapes from thorn bushes or figs from thistles? Even so, every good tree bears good fruit, but a bad tree bears bad fruit. A good tree cannot bear bad fruit, nor can a bad tree bear good fruit. Every tree that does not bear good fruit is cut down and thrown into the fire. Therefore by their fruits you will know them."* (Matthew 7:16-20)

An offspring must always bear resemblance to its progenitor. If you are a good tree, most of your new converts will be good fruits. If you are a bad tree, most of your new converts will be bad fruits.

In many instances, the new converts struggle with vices that are present in the lives of their spiritual parents. You can be endangering your new converts when you tolerate and hide bad habits in your life. Like contagious diseases, they can be transmitted to the lives of your new converts. No matter how much you pretend while around your new converts, and even if they do not notice your inconsistencies, you can still pass those vices to your new converts. We can see examples in the Bible. Rebecca was a con artist, so was her son Jacob. Abraham lied to preserve his life in Egypt, and his son Isaac did the exact same thing.

When you take genuine steps to grow and get rid of bad habits in your life, you are not only doing it for yourself but also for your new converts. The desire for the cares of this world, the deceitfulness of riches, and the desires for other things can be transmitted to our new converts through words, incorrect teachings, beliefs and doctrines, to name a few. This was why Jesus prayed in John 17:19, *"And for their sakes I sanctify Myself, that they also may be sanctified by the truth."*

PURPOSE DRIVEN

Help your new converts to discover their God-given purpose. Most people that succumb to the cares of this world are either devoid of their purpose or lack the passion to diligently pursue it. Help your new converts locate their place in the body of Christ; it will act as a shield from most of the distractions that can make them unfruitful.

Worldly things mainly help people fill a void of futility in their lives. In their quest for meaning, they easily get attracted to worldly things as an avenue to make a mark and secure meaning for their lives. Getting your new converts busy with church activities is not the same as helping them locate their purpose. Activities not born out of purpose will lead to burnout, and eventually, they will become lukewarm. Activities born out of love, however, will keep the new converts passionately seeking God and the actualization of that purpose.

It is more difficult for a person passionately pursuing their God-given purpose to be sidetracked by the cares of this world, the deceitfulness of riches, and the desires for other things. It is said that an idle hand is the devil's workshop. There is some truth to that. Nehemiah was driven to achieve the purpose God had for him and he remained on track. When Solomon was driven to build the temple and his palace, he stayed on track. However, when that goal was achieved, he failed to seek God for another compelling purpose to work towards. As a result of the absence of a compelling purpose, he got distracted and he went astray from serving God.

Jesus Christ was compelled to fulfil His purpose. He said, *"I came to send fire on the earth, and how I wish it were already kindled! But I have a baptism to be baptised with, and how distressed I am till it is accomplished!"* (Luke 12:49-50) A genuine purpose driven person is a focused person.

PRAYER

The cares of this world, the deceitfulness of riches, and the desires for worldly things are temptations from the devil. If older and more experienced believers can fall for those temptations, how much more a new convert. New believers need constant prayers to keep them from the devil's deluge of temptation.

Apostle Peter had a target on his back from the devil. Jesus knew this by revelation. He told Peter, *"Simon, Simon! Indeed, Satan has asked for you, that he may sift you as wheat. But I have prayed for you, that your faith should not fail; and when you have returned to Me, strengthen your brethren."* (Luke 22:31-32) Peter's saving grace was that Jesus prayed for him.

What to Pray For

A skilled sower prays for their converts, before and after the seed has been sown. The Bible tells us to ask and we shall be given (Matthew 7:7 and Luke 11:9); ask God to show you what can cause your new convert to lose their salvation, and pray against such occurrences.

Some Prayer Points:

- Pray that the guilt from past mistakes will not keep your new believers down (Romans 8:1)

- Pray that every plan of Satan to cause your new converts to go astray be foiled (Luke 22:31-32)

- Pray that your new converts will not be unequally yoked like Samson (Judges 16:1-31)

- Pray that the same power of God that enabled the seed to be sown in the hearts of your new converts, will keep them in the faith (1 Peter 1:3-5)

- Pray that your new converts will grow in grace and knowledge of our Lord and Savior Jesus Christ (2 Peter 3:17-18)

Jesus Christ prayed for the disciples He had during His earthly ministry as well as those that will come afterwards. In John 17:6-26, you will see the details of the prayers Jesus prayed for His disciples and all believers. Can you see that a skilled sower does not just sow seeds and leave? Jesus Christ was a skilled sower. He prayed for all His disciples. I believe we are standing today because of the prayer support we received from Jesus, then and now.

Apostle Paul prayed for the believers in the different cities he sowed the word. He prayed for the church in Ephesus:

"Therefore I also, after I heard of your faith in the Lord Jesus and your love for all the saints, do not cease to give thanks for you, making mention of you in my prayers: that the God of our Lord Jesus Christ, the Father of glory, may give to you the spirit of wisdom and revelation in the knowledge of Him, the eyes of your understanding being enlightened; that you may know what is the hope of His calling, what are the riches of the glory of His inheritance in the saints, and what is the exceeding greatness of His power toward us who believe, according to the working of His mighty power which

He worked in Christ when He raised Him from the dead and seated Him at His right hand in the heavenly places, far above all principality and power and might and dominion, and every name that is named, not only in this age but also in that which is to come. And He put all things under His feet, and gave Him to be head over all things to the church, which is His body, the fullness of Him who fills all in all." (Ephesians 1:15-23)

Apostle Paul also prayed for the church in Colossae:

"For this reason we also, since the day we heard it, do not cease to pray for you, and to ask that you may be filled with the knowledge of His will in all wisdom and spiritual understanding; that you may walk worthy of the Lord, fully pleasing Him, being fruitful in every good work and increasing in the knowledge of God; strengthened with all might, according to His glorious power, for all patience and longsuffering with joy; giving thanks to the Father who has qualified us to be partakers of the inheritance of the saints in the light. He has delivered us from the power of darkness and conveyed us into the kingdom of the Son of His love, in whom we have redemption through His blood, the forgiveness of sins." (Colossians 1:9-14)

It is important that you prayerfully identify the areas where your new converts are lacking and bear them up in prayers in those areas. Additionally, it is wise to pray Holy Spirit-inspired prayers, which Jesus Christ and Apostle Paul prayed, over your converts. With this prayer backing, the seed destroying thorns will be destroyed.

7

Some Fell on Good Ground

"But other seed fell on good ground and yielded a crop that sprang up, increased and produced: some thirtyfold, some sixty, and some a hundred."

——Mark 4:8

A skilled sower must know that the true test of a crop's fruitfulness is whether it bears fruit or not. The immediate goal is for the seed to cause the hearer to accept Jesus Christ as their Lord and Saviour. The subsequent goal of the seed is to cause the hearer to lead others to also accept Jesus Christ as their Lord and Saviour.

Jesus explained that the seeds that fell on good ground are *"Those who hear the word, accept it, and bear fruit: some thirtyfold, some sixty, and some a hundred."* (Mark 4:20)

We have explored how a skilled sower can minimize losses from sowing. Now we will explore the ways a skilled sower can increase the yield from their sowing exercise.

INCREASING YOUR YIELD FROM SOW-ING

Thirtyfold, Sixtyfold, Hundredfold

From the parable of the sower, an interesting question arises: why do some fruit bear thirtyfold, some sixty and others a hundred? Can seeds be made to bear more fruit? The clear answer is, yes.

It is good for some seeds to bear thirtyfold or even sixtyfold returns. It is much better, however, to get a hundredfold return. If such an amount of return is available, and it is the will of God for me, I certainly want it.

I read the story of Subrahmanyan Chandrasekhar, a Nobel Laureate in Physics. This Nobel Prize winner was so devoted to his students that in the 1940s, while based at the University of Chicago's Yerkes Observatory, he drove more than 100 miles round-trip each week to teach a class of just two registered students. By 1957, those two students won Nobel Prizes in physics. This is a splendid example of a hundredfold return.

A skilled sower must know how to increase the fruitfulness of his new converts. A skilled sower must encourage them to be seed-sowers themselves. For your seeds sown to be fruitful, note the following factors.

Pruning

One of the ways that God increases our fruitfulness is by pruning. Jesus said, *"Every branch in Me that does not bear fruit He takes away; and every branch that bears fruit He prunes, that it may bear more fruit."* (John 15:2) God the Father is the one that does the pruning.

Pruning is every act of God, designed to increase our effectiveness, efficiency and fruitfulness. Another word for pruning is correction and discipline.

God only corrects those that He loves. Pruning does not feel good in while it is taking place, but it eventually leads to increase in the life of those that yielded to it.

And you have forgotten the exhortation which speaks to you as to sons: "My son, do not despise the chastening of the Lord, nor be discouraged when you are rebuked by Him; For whom

the Lord loves He chastens, and scourges every son whom He receives." If you endure chastening, God deals with you as with sons; for what son is there whom a father does not chasten? But if you are without chastening, of which all have become partakers, then you are illegitimate and not sons. Furthermore, we have had human fathers who corrected us, and we paid them respect. Shall we not much more readily be in subjection to the Father of spirits and live? For they indeed for a few days chastened us as seemed best to them, but He for our profit, that we may be partakers of His holiness. Now no chastening seems to be joyful for the present, but painful; nevertheless, afterward it yields the peaceable fruit of righteousness to those who have been trained by it."
(Hebrews 12:5-11)

A skilled sower confidently and lovingly corrects their new converts. Correcting the new converts is not the same as filling them with guilt. It is lovingly pointing out their mistakes in a manner that is not overwhelming, and proffering a solution to those mistakes. The ultimate goal of the pruning is for increased effectiveness, efficiency and fruitfulness.

Be Patient

Once the seed has been sown, the skilled sower must exercise patience while waiting for the harvest in the lives of their new converts. Jesus Christ was with His disciples for over three years, teaching, training and imparting into them. According to the laws of nature, there is a period of waiting between the time a seed is sown and when the harvest is reaped.

"Therefore be patient, brethren, until the coming of the Lord. See how the farmer waits for the precious fruit of the earth, waiting patiently for it until it receives the early and latter rain." (James 5:7)

We are also encouraged accordingly in Galatians 6:9: *"And let us not grow weary while doing good, for in due season we shall reap if we do not lose heart."* Once you have done your best in sowing the seeds, patiently and thankfully wait for the harvest.

Remember, that it is ultimately God who gives the increase. Your role might have been to plant or to water what someone else had planted; it is in the hands of God to provide the increase.

"I planted, Apollos watered, but God gave the increase." (1 Corinthians 3:6)

Sometimes, you might not see the direct results from your sowing. It will take God sending another person whose responsibility it is to water the seeds you have sown. Hence you might be tempted to think you have wasted your time. Do not be discouraged. Stay focused and immovable. God will not forget your labour of love (Hebrews 6:10). You will reap a bountiful harvest from the seeds you have sown in Jesus' name.

"So then neither he who plants is anything, nor he who waters, but God who gives the increase. Now he who plants and he who waters are one, and each one will receive his own reward according to his own labor." (1 Corinthians 3:7-8)

It takes time to grow anything of value.

Encouragement

No matter how motivated and passionate a new convert is, they will get tired sometimes. There will be times when they will feel like giving up. There will be times when they will be disappointed in their actions, inactions or results. It is the responsibility of the skilled sower to encourage them.

Apostle Paul practiced this regularly. He often wrote epistles filled with encouraging words for his disciples. His epistles are constantly filled with endearing appellations like, "my beloved." These were meant to encourage his co-laborers and let them know that he was on their side. We see this in one of his letters to Timothy, his spiritual son.

"To Timothy, a beloved son: Grace, mercy, and peace from God the Father and Christ Jesus our Lord. I thank God, whom I serve with a pure conscience, as my forefathers did, as without ceasing I remember you in my prayers night and day, greatly desiring to see you, being mindful of your tears, that I may be filled with joy, when I call to remembrance the genuine faith that is in you, which dwelt first in your grandmother Lois and your mother Eunice, and I am persuaded is in you also. Therefore I remind you to stir up the gift of God which is in you through the laying on of my hands." (2 Timothy 1:2-6)

Can you imagine the smile on Timothy's face when he was reading this letter from his spiritual father? He must have been elated. This is not a letter to be thrown away. Whenever he was having bad days, he certainly would have referred back to the letter for encouragement.

Ask God to give you the grace to encourage your new converts. You will need this grace because, at the early stage of their Christian life, they will make lots of mistakes that might not be praiseworthy. Like a toddler, they will soil their pants, struggle to walk, fumble in their speech, display disproportionate emotional responses to events and people. These and much more will be reasons to complain or give up on them. It will help you to remember where God brought you from, and let that fill your heart with hope in God's ability to raise and train your new converts to be fruitful.

Selective Attention

To generate more returns, a skilled sower must be selective on who they focus their attention on. You must make sure that you give the most productive ones the most attention, in order to make them more productive. This might seem counterproductive to you, but it is based on biblical principles. It is not wise to devote the same amount of attention to all your new-converts. Let us examine how Jesus did it.

At some point, Jesus Christ had about five hundred disciples.

"After that He was seen by over five hundred brethren at once, of whom the greater part remain to the present, but some have fallen asleep." (1 Corinthians 15:6)

Out of the five hundred disciples, there was another group of one hundred and twenty.

And in those days Peter stood up in the midst of the disciples (altogether the number of names was about a hundred and twenty), and said, "Men and brethren, this Scripture had to be fulfilled, which the Holy Spirit spoke before by the mouth of David concerning Judas, who became a guide to those who arrested Jesus; for he was numbered with us and obtained a part in this ministry." (Acts 1:15-17)

Out of one hundred and twenty disciples, there was another group of seventy.

After these things the Lord appointed seventy others also, and sent them two by two before His face into every city and place where He Himself was about to go. (Luke 10:1)

Out of the group of seventy, there was a group of twelve disciples.

"And He went up on the mountain and called to Him those He Himself wanted. And they came to Him. Then He appointed twelve, that they might be with Him and that

He might send them out to preach, and to have power to heal sicknesses and to cast out demons: Simon, to whom He gave the name Peter; James the son of Zebedee and John the brother of James, to whom He gave the name Boanerges, that is, "Sons of Thunder"; Andrew, Philip, Bartholomew, Matthew, Thomas, James the son of Alphaeus, Thaddaeus, Simon the Canaanite; and Judas Iscariot, who also betrayed Him. And they went into a house." (Mark 3:13-19)

Out of the group of twelve disciples, Jesus Christ had another group of three.

"Now after six days Jesus took Peter, James, and John, and led them up on a high mountain apart by themselves; and He was transfigured before them." (Mark 9:2)

Then Jesus came with them to a place called Gethsemane, and said to the disciples, "Sit here while I go and pray over there." And He took with Him Peter and the two sons of Zebedee, and He began to be sorrowful and deeply distressed. Then He said to them, "My soul is exceedingly sorrowful, even to death. Stay here and watch with Me." (Matthew 26:36-46)

Jesus Christ shared the most intimate aspects of His ministry with these three people. They also became the most effective of all the disciples.

You might be wondering, am I being asked to show favoritism? Didn't the Bible say that God is not a respecter of persons? In fact, this is in Acts 10:34. It does go on to say in verse 35 that, *"But in every nation whoever fears Him and works righteousness is accepted by Him."* No, I am not asking you to show favouritism. I am simply showing you the pattern Jesus Christ followed. He loved all his disciples, including Judas Iscariot. He gave all His disciples an equal opportunity to draw closer to Him, but He gave more attention to those that actually drew closer.

Take note of those who ask more questions and are engaged. It is typically a sign exhibited by those that will be very fruitful. Give them more of your time and attention.

Epilogue

Engaging in an activity in God's name without involving Him in it is counterintuitive.

I encourage you to meditate on Isaiah 28:23-29. This is God Himself advising us to take heed to His advice. God is an excellent teacher. He knows the end from the beginning. You are not boring Him by asking as many questions as possible. Let Him be the one to guide your evangelistic efforts, so you do not end up wasting your time and energy. Our Heavenly Father is wonderful in counsel and excellent in guidance.

Give ear and hear my voice, listen and hear my speech. Does the plowman keep plowing all day to sow? Does he keep turning his soil and breaking the clods? When he has leveled its surface, does he not sow the black cummin and scatter the cummin, plant the wheat in rows, the barley in the appointed place, and the spelt in its place? For He instructs him in right judgment, His God teaches him. For the black cummin is not threshed with a threshing-sledge, nor is a cartwheel rolled over the cummin; but the black cummin is beaten out with a stick, and the cummin with a rod. Bread flour must be ground; Therefore he does not thresh it forever, break it with his cartwheel, or crush it with his horsemen. This also comes from the Lord of hosts, who is wonderful in counsel and excellent in guidance. (Isaiah 28:23-29)

As you go out to sow, both through hunting or fishing, may God crown your efforts with success. May you not be weary in doing good. May you see and enjoy the fruits of your labour in Jesus' name.

God bless you!

Contact the Author

I know without a doubt that this book has been a blessing to you. I am looking forward to hearing your testimony.

You can stay connected with me through the following platforms:

Instagram: e.adewusi | **Youtube:** Emmanuel Adewusi
Website: emmanueladewusi.org

Review the Book

A Sinner's Prayer

Dear Heavenly Father,

I come to You in the Name of Jesus Christ.

You said in Your Word, "Whosoever shall call upon the name of the Lord shall be saved." (Romans 10:13) I am calling on Your Name, so I know You have saved me now.

You also said that "if you confess with your mouth the Lord Jesus and believe in your heart that God has raised Him from the dead, you will be saved. For with the heart one believes unto righteousness, and with the mouth, confession is made unto salvation." (Romans 10:9-10) I believe in my heart Jesus Christ is the Son of God. I believe that He was raised from the dead for my justification, and I confess Him now as my Lord and Saviour.

Thank you, Lord, because now, I am saved!

Thank You, Lord, because I know you have heard my prayer. Thank You, Lord, because I am now born again.

Signed _____

Date _____

About the Author

Apostle Emmanuel Adewusi is the Founding and Lead Pastor of Cornerstone Christian Church of God.

Called into ministry with the mandate to "bring restoration and transformation to all by teaching, preaching, and demonstrating the Gospel of Jesus Christ," he is passionate about seeing lives restored and transformed as God intended from the beginning of creation. He has a zeal for the full counsel of the Word of God, fellowship with the Holy Spirit, and being under spiritual authority.

He authored the books *"Now That You Are Born Again, What Next?"*, *"The Blessings of Being Under Spiritual Authority,"* *"A Disciplined Life,"* *"The Enlightened Believer,"* *"The Skilled Sower,"* and other impactful titles. He has also released an album titled *"Divine Encounter"* and many more on the way.

Emmanuel Adewusi is joyfully married to his wife, Ibukun Adewusi, and together, they are building a thriving Christ-centered family.